Talented TAILS
Up Close

Animal
Bodies
**UP
CLOSE**

Enslow Elementary
an imprint of
Enslow Publishers, Inc.
40 Industrial Road
Box 398
Berkeley Heights, NJ 07922
USA
http://www.enslow.com

Melissa Stewart

CONTENTS

WORDS TO KNOW

predator (PREH duh tur)— An animal that hunts and kills other animals for food.

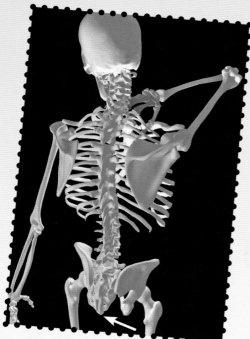

tailbone (TEYL bohn)—A small triangle-shaped bone at the bottom of a person's backbone.

SPIDER MONKEY

Animals use their tails in all kinds of ways. This monkey uses its tail like an extra hand. The tail can pick fruit off of trees. It also helps the monkey swing from branch to branch.

4

BEAVER

Look at this beaver's big, flat tail. It is perfect for steering through the water.

When a beaver feels scared, it slaps its tail against the water. The loud sound warns other beavers.

EASTERN DIAMONDBACK RATTLESNAKE

What does this snake do when there is danger? It shakes the tip of its tail. The rattling sound sends out a message. It says, "Stay away. I'm full of poison."

UP CLOSE

GREAT WHITE SHARK

A shark is a fish. Its strong tail pushes it through the water. A shark's tail bends from side to side as it swims through the sea.

GRAY SQUIRREL

How does a squirrel use its tail?
To balance on tree branches.
And to land safely when it jumps.

But that's not all the tail does. When it
rains, a squirrel uses its tail like an umbrella.
On cold nights, the tail makes a good blanket.

PLATYPUS

A platypus (PLAH tih puhs) stores fat in its tail. It uses the fat when it can't find food. The tail makes a good paddle, too. It helps a platypus swim.

After a female lays eggs, she curls her tail around them. That's how she keeps the eggs warm.

BLUE-TAILED SKINK

How does this lizard stay safe?
It has a trick. When **predators** attack,
the skink's bright blue tail falls off. And it
keeps on wriggling! That gives the skink
a chance to run away.

YOUR TAILBONE

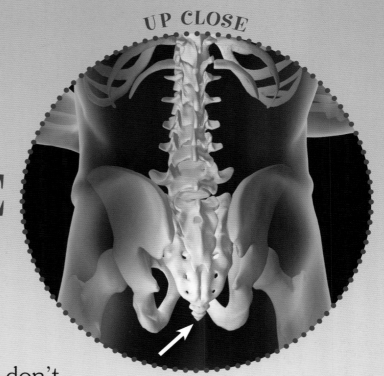

You are an animal too. You don't have a tail, but you do have a **tailbone**. It helps you balance when you are sitting down.

18

GUESSING GAME

1. **A kangaroo's tail . . .**

2. **A scorpion's tail . . .**

3. **A giraffe's tail . . .**

4. **A peacock's tail . . .**

A. **brushes insects off its back.**

B. **attracts mates.**

C. **balances its body.**

D. **stings attackers.**

Write your answers on a piece of paper. Please do not write in this book!

See answers on page 24.

kangaroo

scorpion

giraffe

peacock

21

LEARN MORE

Books

Bozzo, Linda. *Amazing Animal Tails.* New York: PowerKids Press, 2008.

Hall, Peg. *Whose Tail Is This?* Mankato, Minn.: Picture Window Books, 2007.

Jenkins, Steve and Robin Page. *What Do You Do with a Tail Like This?* Boston: Houghton Mifflin, 2003.

Leake, Diyan. *Tails.* Chicago: Heinemann-Raintree, 2007.

WEB SITES

A Tale of Tails

http://www.highlightskids.
com/Science/Stories/
SS0306_taleofTails.asp

Talking Tails

http://scienceprojectideasforkids.
com/2009/taking-tails/

INDEX

Note to Parents and Teachers: The *Animal Bodies Up Close* series supports the National Science Education Standards for K–4 science. The Words to Know section introduces subject-specific vocabulary words, including pronunciation and definitions. Early readers may need help with these new words.

Enslow Elementary, an imprint of Enslow Publishers, Inc.

Enslow Elementary® is a registered trademark of Enslow Publishers, Inc.

Copyright © 2012 by Melissa Stewart

Library of Congress Cataloging-in-Publication Data

Stewart, Melissa.

Talented tails up close / Melissa Stewart.

p. cm. — (Animal bodies up close)

Includes index.

Summary: "Discover how different animals use their tails to keep their balance, swim, and more"—Provided by publisher.

ISBN 978-0-7660-3893-6

1. Tail—Juvenile literature. I. Title.

QL950.6.S74 2011

591.47—dc22

2011003340

Future editions:

Paperback ISBN 978-1-4644-0082-7

ePUB ISBN 978-1-4645-0989-6

PDF ISBN 978-1-4646-0989-3

Printed in the China

012012 Leo Paper Group, Heshan City, Guangdong, China

10 9 8 7 6 5 4 3 2 1

Photo Credits: © 2011 Photos.com, a division of Getty Images, pp. 3 (tailbone), 8, 20, 21; Alamy: © Kunst and Scheidulin, p. 6, © Gerard Lacz, p. 10; Ardea.com: © Brian Bevan, p. 13, © Hans + Judy Beste, p. 15; Photolibrary: Bios, pp. 4, 5, 14, Design Pics Inc., p. 16; iStockphoto.com: © Andrew Howe, p. 12, © Thomas Voss, p. 21 (giraffe), © Todd Winner, p. 11; Minden Pictures: © Michael Quinton, p. 7, © Pete Oxford, p. 9, Tony Heald/npl, p. 3 (predator); © Osf/Cheng, W./Animals Animals - Earth Scenes, p. 17; Shutterstock.com, pp. 1, 2, 21 (kangaroo, scorpion, peacock), 23.

Cover Photo: Shutterstock.com

Series Literacy Consultant:
Allan A. De Fina, PhD
Dean, College of Education
Professor of Literacy Education
New Jersey City University
Past President of the New Jersey Reading
Association

Science Consultant:
Helen Hess, PhD
Professor of Biology
College of the Atlantic
Bar Harbor, Maine

Answers to the Guessing Game

Kangaroo: C. balances its body.

Scorpion: D. stings attackers.

Giraffe: A. brushes insects off its back.

Peacock: B. attracts mates.